THE Animal HALL OF FAME
Volume 2 By TJ Rob

The Strongest, Longest, Smartest, Highest Flying, Deepest Living, Biggest Eater and MORE...

The ANIMAL HALL OF FAME — Volume 2

By TJ Rob

Animal Feats and Records Series — Volume 2

Copyright Text TJ Rob, 2016
All rights reserved. No part of the book may be reproduced in any form without permission in writing from the author. Reviewers may quote brief passages in review.
ISBN 978-1-988695-30-3

Disclaimer:
No part of this book may be reproduced in any form or by any means, mechanical or electronic, including photocopying or recording, or by an information storage and retrieval system, or transmitted by email without permission in writing from the publisher. This book is for entertainment purposes only. The views expressed are those of author alone.

Published by:
TJ Rob
Suite 609
440-10816 Macleod Trail SE
Calgary, AB T2J 5N8 www.TJRob.com

Photo Credits: Images used under license from Shutterstock.com, Flickr.com, Creative Commons and Public Domain:
Cover page, Angela Waye/Shutterstock.com; Back Page, Jenn Kahalau Photography/Flickr.com; pg. 1, Angela Waye/Shutterstock.com; pg. 4, D Ramey Logan/CC BY-SA 3.0 via Wikimedia Commons; pg. 5, Gregrory Smith/Flickr.com; pg. 6, Andi Gentsch/Flickr.com; pg. 7, Jeremy T. Hetzel /Flickr.com; pg. 8, Bartkusa/Flickr.com; pg. 10, DanielPerdigueroPhoto/Shutterstock.com; pg. 11, sysasya photography/Shutterstock.com; pg. 12, Creative Commons; pg. 13, By NOAA Photo Library - anim1754, Public Domain; pg. 14, Rudmer Zwerver/Shutterstock.com; pg. 15, Leigh Gregg/Shutterstock.com; pg. 16, Menno Schaefer/Shutterstock.com; pg. 17, Sergey Ryzhov/Shutterstock.com; pg. 17, Rafal Cichawa/Shutterstock.com; pg. 18, Original photo by Arthur A. Allen, coloured version by Jerry A. Payne - Image 2513013 Forestry Images; pg. 19, Eduard Kyslynskyy/Shutterstock.com; pg. 20, Dennis W. Donohue/Shutterstock.com; pg. 21, Liam Quinn/CC BY-SA 2.0 via Wikimedia Commons; pg. 22, nanka/Shutterstock.com; pg. 22, Barsan ATTILA/Shutterstock.com; pg. 23, EastVillage Images/Shutterstock.com; pg. 24, Jo-anne Hounsom/Shutterstock.com; pg. 25, Estrada Anton/Shutterstock.com; pg. 25, NinaM/Shutterstock.com; pg. 26, Sergey Uryadnikov/Shutterstock.com; pg. 26, Alicia Chelini/Shutterstock.com; pg. 27, Audrey Snider-Bell/Shutterstock.com; pg. 28, Cuson/Shutterstock.com; pg. 29, Stacey Newman/Shutterstock.com; pg. 30, Joseph Wolf [Public domain], via Wikimedia Commons ; pg. 33, Kris Wiktor/Shutterstock.com; pg. 34, asawinimages/Shutterstock.com; pg. 35, Darkroomillusions/Flickr.com; pg. 36, Kjersti Joergensen/Shutterstock.com; pg. 38, Hawk777/Shutterstock.com; pg. 38, boyphare/Shutterstock.com; pg. 38, yanikap/Shutterstock.com; pg. 41, Rob Francis/Shutterstock.com

TABLE OF CONTENTS

	Page
The Strongest in Sheer Power	4
The Strongest in Size and Weight	6
The Longest Overall	9
The Smartest	10
The Highest Flying	11
The Deepest Living Creature	12
The Biggest Eater	13
The Hungriest Animal	14
The Longest Animal Pregnancy	15
The Longest Migration	16
The Biggest Eggs	17
The Rarest	18
The Biggest Nest	20
The Softest Fur	22
The Biggest Herds	23
The Biggest Teeth	24
The Most Teeth	25
The Biggest Spider	27
The Most Shocking	28
The Smelliest	30
The Best Camouflage	32
The Best Animal Mothers	35
The Most Successful Hunters	39
The Bravest and Most Fearless	40
Please leave a review and Other EXCITING books by TJ Rob	42

The Strongest in Sheer Power
The BLUE WHALE

The biggest and heaviest creature EVER to have lived on planet Earth is also maybe the STRONGEST!

With a weight of 400,000 pounds (181,000 kg) and a length of 100 feet (30 meters), Blue Whales need to have enormous strength to move their size and weight around. This gives them the title of brute strength champion in the Animal Kingdom.

They have been known to flip over boats of more than 60,000 pounds (27,000 kg) with ease using their tails.

The Strongest by Size and Weight

The DUNG BEETLE

For its size and its weight the Dung Beetle is the STRONGEST!

Not only is the Dung Beetle the world's strongest insect but it is also the strongest animal on the planet compared to its body weight.

Dung Beetles have an average length of only 1.75 inches (4.5 cm) and weight of .75 ounces (21.25 gm).

They are so strong that they can lift and pull 1,140 times their own body weight.

This would be the equivalent to 1 average person pulling 6 double-decker buses loaded full of people — or the same as 1 human lifting 180,000 pounds (81,650 kg)!

No other animal on Earth can push and pull over 1,000 times its own body weight.

The Longest Overall

The LION's MANE JELLYFISH

Also known as the Giant Jellyfish or Hair Jellyfish, it is the largest of all Jellyfish.

The largest one ever caught had a bell measuring 7 feet 6 inches (2.3 meters) and had tentacles 121 feet (36.9 meters) long. That is longer than a Blue Whale.

Their tentacles are arranged in 8 sets. Each set can have up to 150 individual tentacles. That's up to 1,200 tentacles in total.

The Lion's Mane Jellyfish is poisonous and can be fatal to humans. But don't expect to find any.

They love deep water and it must be very cold—like the Northern Atlantic and the Artic Oceans.

The Smartest
The CHIMPANZEE

Chimpanzees or Chimps are able to recognize themselves in a mirror. They are able to show a range of emotions similar to humans, such as caring or mourning.

They learn from their surroundings and make tools to protect themselves and to hunt.

Like humans, they cooperate with one another and plan ahead when hunting. They are good communicators.

Some have been taught to understand words and to communicate with humans using symbols and signs.

Chimps are the closest living relatives to humans in the animal kingdom. They share 98% of the same DNA as humans.

They are found in Central Africa and West Africa. Males are up to 4 feet (1.2 meters) tall and weigh as much as 150 pounds (70 kg). Females are a bit smaller. Chimps live from 33 to 37 years in the wild and have lived up to 60 years in captivity.

The Highest Flying
RUPPELL'S GRIFFON VULTURE

Named after Eduard Ruppell, a 19th-century German explorer, collector and zoologist.

A Ruppell's Griffon Vulture was measured flying at 37,000 feet (11,277 meters) above sea level. This is 7 miles (11.25 km) straight up — more than 1.5 miles (2.4 km) higher than the top of Mount Everest.

These Vultures live throughout Central and Western Africa.

They have a lifespan of 40 to 50 years.

They feed mainly off dead and decaying animals.

These large birds weigh from 14 to 20 pounds (6.35 to 9 kg). They have a huge wingspan of 7.5 to 8.5 feet (2.3 to 2.6 meters) wide. This allows them to fly very high and soar for up to 6 hours at a time.

The Deepest Living Creature
The HADAL SNAILFISH

The Hadal Snailfish is a creature that lives at one of the greatest depths on Earth. These images were taken at a depth of 26,722 feet (8,145 meters), photographed by a hidden camera.

These fish survive at depths that scientists thought was not possible.

At these depths, there is no light and the water is so cold it is permanently just a few degrees above freezing.

Also, the pressure at these great depths is crushing. The pressure at these depths would be like having the weight of 50 Jumbo Jets pressing on your chest.

Navy submarines can only go as deep as 2,500 feet underwater before the pressure would crush them like us crushing an empty soda can.

The Biggest Eater
The BLUE WHALE

The Blue Whale is the largest creature on Earth and it has the largest appetite. It can eat as many as 40 million Krill per day.

Krill are tiny shrimp-like creatures. 40 million Krill can weigh close to 8,000 pounds (3,600 kg) and this huge beast eats this much every day!

Krill live in huge swarms of millions of creatures. Blue Whales mostly find the Krill at depths of 300 feet (100 meters).

The amount that a Blue Whale eats in 1 day could feed 1,450 Americans for the day.

Baby Blue Whales drink their mother's milk during the first 6 – 18 months of life instead of eating Krill. A baby can drink as much as 150 gallons (570 liters) of milk per day during its first year.

The Hungriest Animal
The AMERICAN PYGMY SHREW

The American Pygmy Shrew is tiny. Just 2.0 inches (5 cm) long and weighing about 0.071 to 0.088 ounces (2 to 4.5 g). Even though it is so small it eats non-stop throughout the day.

A Blue Whale eats a lot more food, but this little Shrew eats 3 times its body weight every day to stay alive.

A Blue Whale does not even eat 2% of its body weight every day. We humans eat only 2% to 4% of our body weight every day.

The Pygmy Shrew burns up its food so fast that it must eat every 15 to 20 minutes. An hour without food could mean its death. Because it needs food so often, this Shrew only sleeps for a few minutes at a time.

American Pygmy Shrews eat mainly insects. They live across Canada, Alaska and the North East USA.

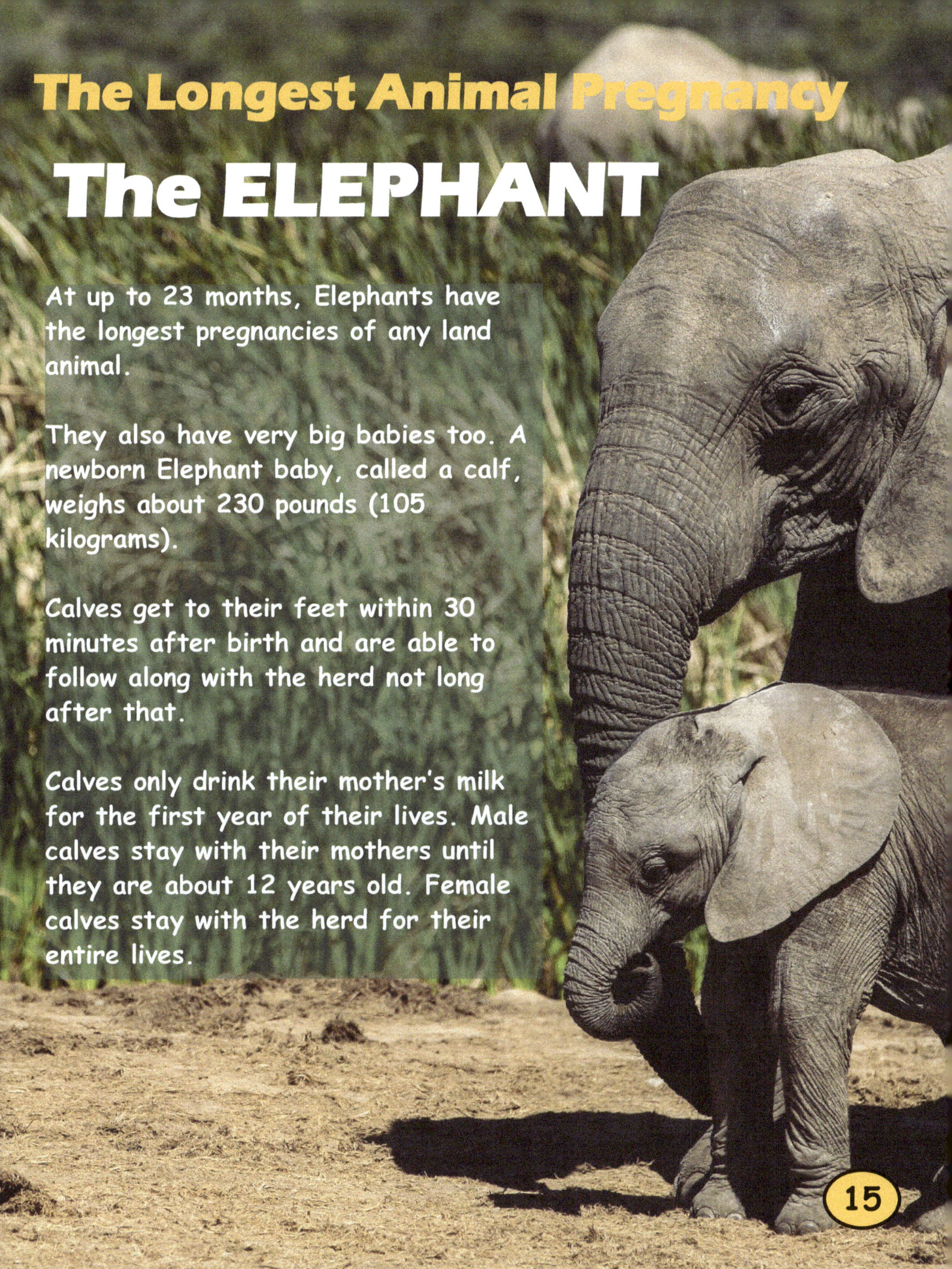

The Longest Animal Pregnancy
The ELEPHANT

At up to 23 months, Elephants have the longest pregnancies of any land animal.

They also have very big babies too. A newborn Elephant baby, called a calf, weighs about 230 pounds (105 kilograms).

Calves get to their feet within 30 minutes after birth and are able to follow along with the herd not long after that.

Calves only drink their mother's milk for the first year of their lives. Male calves stay with their mothers until they are about 12 years old. Female calves stay with the herd for their entire lives.

The Longest Migration
The ARTIC TERN

Many different species migrate long distances each year to breed or to find food.

The Artic Tern holds the record for the longest migration recorded by any animal. It flies from its Arctic breeding grounds to the Antarctic and back again each year.

It follows a zig-zag route of about 44,000 miles (70,800 km) every year.

The long journey gives this bird two summers per year and more daylight than any other creature on the planet.

Arctic terns are medium-sized birds. They have a length of 11-15 inches 28-39 cm) and a wingspan of 26-30 inches (65-75 cm).

With an average lifespan of 30 years, the Artic Tern covers about 1.5 million miles in its lifetime — about the same distance as going to the Moon and back 3 times.

The Biggest Eggs
The OSTRICH EGG

The world's biggest bird lays the world's biggest eggs. On average, Ostrich eggs are 6 inches (15 cm) long, 5.1 inches (13 cm) wide, and weigh 3.1 pounds (1.4 kg).

1 Ostrich egg is the equivalent of 25 Chicken eggs — one huge omelet.

Ostriches weigh 140 – 290 pounds (63.5-131.5 kg) and measure 6 – 9 feet (1.8-2.7 meters) in height.

Ostrich wings reach a span of about 7 feet (2 meters) and are used in mating displays and to shade chicks. They are not able to fly, but they can run really fast.

Ostriches mainly eat seeds, shrubs, grass, fruit, flowers and sometimes insects such as locusts. They are found in Africa in the wild.

The Rarest

The IVORY-BILLED WOODPECKER

The Ivory-Billed Woodpecker is the largest Woodpecker in the world, at roughly 20 inches (51 cm) long and 30 inches (76 cm) in wingspan.

It is thought that it lives in the forests of the South Eastern USA.

Its numbers are so low — it may even already be extinct.
No modern photos exist of this bird. This picture is a hand colored photo, taken in 1935.

This bird is on the Critically Endangered Species list.

The Rarest
The AMUR LEOPARD

The Amur Leopard is a very rare Leopard subspecies that lives only in the remote and snowy northern forests of Eastern Russia.

Poached for its beautiful, spotted fur only 70 adults remain in the wild. The Amur Leopard is the most endangered big cat in the world.

The Amur Leopard is a nocturnal creature that lives and hunts alone. It has a unique coat with widely spaced rosettes with thick black borders — makes it easy to identify from other species of Leopard.

In the summer its coat is short, but in the winter it thickens up to 2.75 inches (7 cm) long to help keep it warm.

The Biggest Nest
The BALD EAGLE Nest

The biggest nest ever found was in St. Petersburg Florida in 1963. The nest was made by a pair of Bald Eagles. The nest measured 9.5 feet wide (2.9 meters) wide and 20 feet (6 meters) deep. It weighed more than 4,410 pounds (2,000 kg).

A pair of eagles starts working on their nest 1 to 3 months before the female lays the first egg.

Bald Eagles like to build their nests close to water.

When you think of a nest, you think of sticks and twigs. You don't think of a nest that weighs more than 1,000 pounds (453 kg).

Eagles keep adding sticks to the nest and they continue to build on to the same nest for many years. That is how their nests grow so big.

They interweave the sticks and fill in spaces with grasses, mosses and other fibers. To soften the bottom, parents line the nest with their own feathers.

The Softest Fur
The CHINCHILA

Chinchillas are medium sized rodents found in the wild in the Andes Mountains in South America. They are also kept as pets.

Chinchillas get their name from the South American tribe called "Chinchas" — who hunt them for their very thick fur.

Their fur is so thick it is considered the softest fur in the world.

Humans have only 1 hair per hair follicle. Chinchillas have about 60 to 70 fine hairs growing from each follicle.

Chinchillas are a nocturnal species and hide during the day time.

They grow to about 12 inches (30 cm) in height and weigh between 1.2 - 4 pounds (0.6 – 1.8 kg). The female is bigger than the male.

The Biggest Herds
The Great WILDEBEEST Migration

Nowhere in the world is there a movement of animals as big as the Great Wildebeest Migration. Over 1.7 million Wildebeest migrate from the Serengeti National Park in Tanzania to the greener pastures of the Maasai Mara National Reserve in Kenya during July through to October.

Wildebeest are a type of antelope. They are also called "Gnus". Wildebeest do look a lot like some breeds of cattle.

The exact start of migration cannot be predicted. It depends on the rainfall and availability of food.

By October the Wildebeest herds are again migrating South, returning to the short-grass plains of the Southern Serengeti in November.

The Biggest Teeth
The AFRICAN ELEPHANT

Elephants have the biggest teeth of all animals. An Elephant's tusks are actually long incisors and are no different from other teeth.

One third of the tusk is actually hidden from view, buried deep inside the Elephant's head. This part of the tusk is a cavity made up of tissue, blood and nerves.

The visible ivory part of the tusk is made of dentine with an outer layer of enamel. The tusk is hollow at the top but becomes solid towards the tips.

An Elephant's tusks never stop growing so some old males have huge tusks. Like a tooth, if a tusk is broken off at the root it cannot grow back again.

Like humans that are either left or right handed, Elephants prefer one tusk over the other.

The Most Teeth   The SNAIL

Snails have the most teeth in the Animal kingdom. Most snails have thousands of microscopic teeth that are actually found on the tongue of the snail. The snail's tongue is called a radula.

The radula works like a file, ripping food into small pieces. A snail may have over 25,000 teeth on its radula.

Most Snails eat plants, fruits, vegetables and algae.

The Most Teeth
The SHORT-BEAKED COMMON DOLPHIN

Most Dolphins don't even use their teeth to chew. They swallow their prey whole. They only use their teeth to grab hold of their prey.

A Short-Beaked Common Dolphin has the most teeth of any mammal. This dolphin usually has around 240 cone-shaped teeth that are approximately 0.5 inch (1.25 cm) in diameter.

They are spaced evenly apart and designed to interlock. This makes it easy to capture prey.

Like humans, when a Dolphin loses a tooth, it is gone for good. It cannot grow back.

The Biggest SPIDER

The GOLIATH BIRD-EATING TARANTULA

The biggest Spider in the world is the Goliath Bird-Eating Tarantula. This spider is large enough to eat birds, but mainly eats Earthworms and Toads.

The Goliath can reach up to 1 foot (30 cm) in body length and has 1 inch (2.5 cm) long fangs.

The Goliath has tiny hairs on its body that it shoots at whoever is threatening it.

They also carry venom in their fangs and will bite when threatened. Their venom is relatively harmless and its effects are similar to a Wasp's sting.

The Goliath rubs its legs together to make a hissing noise and it can be heard up to 15 feet (4.5 meters) away.

The Goliath Bird-Eating Tarantula lives in the rainforests of South America.

People also keep them as pets. They have a lifespan of 3 to 6 years.

The Most Shocking
The ELECTRIC EEL

Although they look like Eels, the Electric Eel is not one. It is a type of Electric Knifefish.

Electric Eels are mostly blind and use a radar system of electrical pulses to navigate and find food. Like other electric fish, they produce low-voltage pulses to feel out their environment.

They are famous for their ability to generate extremely high-voltage shocks which stun or kill prey. This is how they defend themselves.

Electric Eels can grow to over eight feet (2.4 meters) long and weigh nearly 50 pounds (22.7 kilograms).

A large Electric Eel can generate a shock of over 860 volts, more than 7 times the voltage of a wall socket.

Human deaths from an Electric Eel are rare.

Electric Eels live in the Amazon and Orinoco Rivers in South America.

The Smelliest
The STRIPED POLECAT

The Striped Polecat, also known as the Zorilla, is a member of the Weasel family. It looks a lot like a Skunk. It is thought to be the world's smelliest creature.

The Skunk is more famous, but the Striped Polecat's spray is much stronger and smellier.

Its anal glands can be smelled from a half a mile (0.8 km) away. That's over 7 football fields.

Like a Skunk, the Striped Polecat can shoot smelly secretions from its anal glands to protect against predators. The anal spray is so powerful that it temporarily blinds the predator resulting in an intense burning sensation.

If the predator doesn't back down from the initial burn, then the smell will definitely do the job.

They are very aggressive and territorial animals. A single animal has been known to keep a pride of full-grown Lions at bay.

This smelly creature lives in Africa.

The Best Camouflage
The LEAFY SEADRAGON

The Leafy Seadragon gets its name from leaf-like protrusions all over its body. These act as camouflage. It is also called Glauert's Seadragon.

It is found in water along the Southern and Western coasts of Australia.

These creatures grow to between 8 to 10 inches (20 to 25 cm) long. They eat plankton.

The Leafy Seadragon has become an endangered animal and is now protected by the Australian Government.

These animals cannot hold onto things like seagrass with their tails. In bad storms they often get washed up onto dry land.

Leafy Seadragons have a lifespan of 5 to 10 years.

The Best Camouflage
The WALKING LEAF

One of natures best camouflaged animals is the Walking Leaf. Also called the Leaf Insect.

The Walking Leaf lives in South Asia and Australia.

Its amazing natural camouflage makes it virtually invisible in wooded areas. This allows it to hide from predators.

It also allows its own prey to come to it while remaining hidden.

A Walking Leaf is able to sway back and forth like a real leaf blowing in the wind.

These insects may have existed on Earth for over 45 million years.

The Best Animal Mothers
ELEPHANTS

Elephant mothers and babies have the closest relationships of any animal on earth.

After the longest pregnancy of any mammal (up to 23 months), Elephant mothers nurse their calves for 4 - 6 years.

Even after they are weaned, Elephant calves stay with their mothers for about 12 years.

Once a baby is born, the other females in the herd all help with the rearing of the young calf.

Elephant mothers help their babies walk, pick them up when they fall, find them when they stray, bathe them and nurture them constantly. Even after they can feed and fend for themselves, female Elephants stay close to their mothers for life.

The Best Animal Mothers
ORANGUTANS

Orangutan babies are fully dependent on their mothers until they are 2 years old.

For the first 4 months, a baby will never break physical contact with its mother, clinging to her belly the whole time.

Each night, mom makes a nest that she and baby will cuddle in all night.

Even as they get older, Orangutans are highly attached to mom. They even breastfeed until they are around 5 years old — making them the species with the longest dependence period.

The moms stay with their young for 6 to 7 years, teaching them where to find food, what and how to eat and how to build a sleeping nest.

Female Orangutans are known to visit their mothers until they reach the age of 15 or 16.

The Most Successful Hunters
DRAGONFLIES

A Dragonfly captures 90 to 95% of the prey it hunts. It is the champion hunter of all animals.

Lions catch their prey less than 25% of the time. Great White Sharks do a bit better — 50%. African Wild Dogs are even better — 67% (2 out of every 3 tries). Cougars catch 8 out of every 10, or are 80% successful at capturing their prey.

What is the Dragonfly's secret to success?

Dragonflies do not chase their prey. They ambush their prey from behind.

Dragonflies have the best vision in the insect world with a 360 degree view.

They also have incredible flying abilities in the air. Their four wings move separately and each wing can be rotated on its own.

Dragonflies catch other flying insects, like midges and mosquitoes.

The Bravest and Most Fearless
THE HONEY BADGER

Honey badgers are small animals, similar in size to a medium sized dog. They are between 23 and 39 inches (60 and 100 cm) long and weigh between 11 to 33 pounds (5 and 15 kg).

Honey Badgers will attack animals larger than themselves — Porcupines, Snakes, Buck, Lions and even small Crocodiles.

Honey Badgers have a great sense of smell. They love honey, breaking into Bee hives using their long powerful claws. They do not fear getting stung.

They hunt and eat some of the most venomous Snakes in Africa. They are not affected by snake venom. At worst it will knock them out for a short time but they soon recover.

These animals have very sharp teeth and strong jaws to crush bones and tortoise shells. Their skin is so tough that arrows and spears cannot get through it.

Not just very tough, they are super clever as well. They use tools to find food.

Honey Badgers live throughout Africa and some parts of Asia like Eastern Iran, Southern Iraq, Pakistan and Western India.

THANKS FOR READING!

Please leave a review at the website where you bought this book and tell others what you liked about it.

Visit www.TJRob.com for a FREE eBook and to see TJ Rob's other exciting books

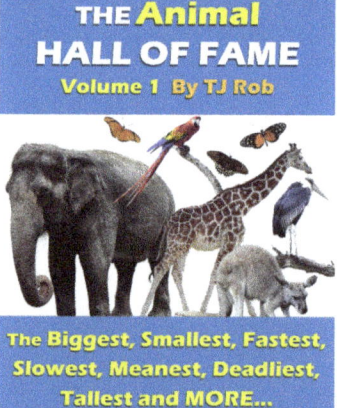
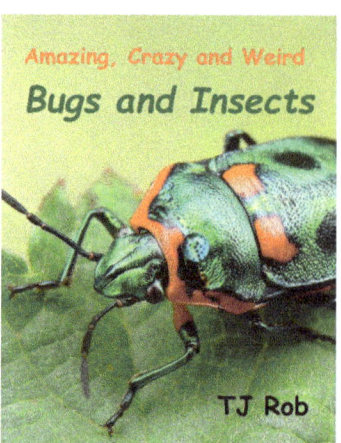
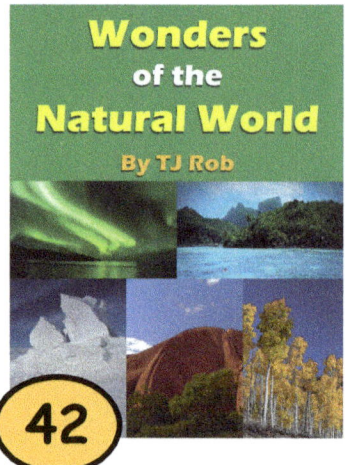
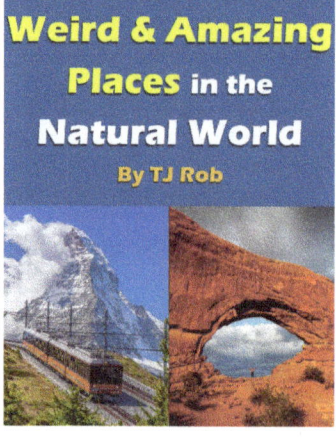

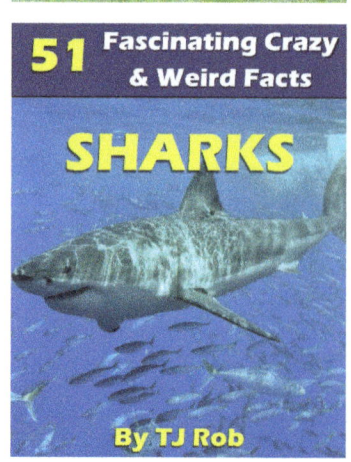

www.ingramcontent.com/pod-product-compliance
Lightning Source LLC
Chambersburg PA
CBHW040004080526
44586CB00027B/2882